Chysauster and Carn Euny

CORNWALL

PATRICIA M L CHRISTIE PhD, FSA

The west of Cornwall is rich in prehistory. Man and nature have combined to produce mysterious stone circles, standing stones, burial chambers and ancient villages. Two of these villages are described in this guidebook, Chysauster and Carn Euny. Chysauster was occupied mainly in the Romano-British period. Carn Euny had a longer period of occupation from about 500BC to as late as AD400. Both comprise groups of stone-walled homesteads known as 'courtyard houses'. Each house had an open central courtyard surrounded by a number of rooms roofed with turf or thatch. A feature of both villages was an underground stone-walled passage known as a 'fogou', which may have served as a store, a refuge or even a religious or cult centre.

ENGLISH HERITAGE · LONDON

Contents

Chysauster

3 INTRODUCTION
3 The Site
4 History
4 Field System
5 Dating
6 Environment and Economy

10 DESCRIPTION AND TOUR
10 General description of the houses
11 Finds
12 Tour of the houses
12 House 5
14 House 3
15 House 1
16 House 2
16 House 4
17 House 6
20 House 8
20 House 7
22 House 9
22 Fogou

10 PLAN OF CHYSAUSTER

Carn Euny

23 INTRODUCTION
24 The Settlement
25 Fogou
27 Dating
28 Environmental background
29 Economy

27 CHRONOLOGICAL CHART

31 DESCRIPTION AND TOUR
31 General description of the houses
33 House II
34 House I
35 Fogou
39 Houses A and B
41 House A1
41 House E
42 House F
42 House III
43 House IV
43 Cottage

32 PLAN OF CARN EUNY

45 FURTHER READING

Pottery, reconstructions and plans were drawn by Judith Dobie of English Heritage

Unless otherwise stated illustrations are copyright English Heritage and the photographs were taken by the English Heritage Photographic Section (Photo Library: 0207-973 3338)

Published by English Heritage
Waterhouse Square, 138-142 Holborn, London, EC1N 2NH
© Copyright English Heritage 1993
First published by English Heritage 1993, second edition 1997, reprinted 2000, 2002, 2004, 2007
Previously published separately as 'Chysauster Ancient Village' (English Heritage 1987) and 'Carn Euny Prehistoric Village' (HMSO 1983)
Printed in England by Hawthornes
05/07, C4O, 0563, 38776, J345, FA4898
ISBN 1 85074 680 X

Chysauster

Chysauster Ancient Village : a reconstruction showing Houses 4 and 6

The site

Chysauster is one of a number of ancient stone-walled villages to be found in the West Penwith area of Cornwall. Although these settlements share many features in common, excavation has shown that together they span a considerable period of time. Some show occupation starting in the last centuries BC, during the local Iron Age, and continuing through the period when the Romans were occupying much of Britain.

One such site is Carn Euny (described in the second half of this book on page 23) which has revealed several phases of occupation and development, involving a great deal of adaptation and rebuilding over some 700 years.

Other settlements, notably Chysauster, appear to have been constructed during the Roman period and to have been occupied for a relatively short time, with little major rebuilding, which probably accounts for the better state of the houses. However there is also evidence of earlier Iron Age activity at Chysauster in the form of pottery, though no houses of this period have yet been identified.

These ancient settlements vary in size, form and state of preservation, but they share important features, chief among them being a specialised type of compartmented house-form peculiar to west Cornwall, but not unlike some broadly contemporary houses found in Wales and elsewhere in the highland zone of Britain. These 'courtyard houses', as they are known in Cornwall, are confined to the Land's End peninsula and the Isles of Scilly. A detailed description is given on page 10.

They are situated between 350ft (106m) and 600ft (189m) above sea level on granite uplands rich in antiquities. Most are within sight of a hill-top fort of Iron Age date with which they may at some time have had political or social association; in the case of Chysauster this is Castle-an-Dinas, one mile (1.6km) to the east. Among these villages Chysauster appears to be exceptional both in its regular lay-out and standardised house-form.

Associated with several of these sites, though with the earlier phases of their use, are the underground structures (souterrains) locally known as 'fogous' after a late Cornish word meaning cave. Like the sites to which they may be linked, these fogous vary in their state of preservation. That at Chysauster, for example, is in a ruinous state and remains to be excavated, so that access is limited. The fine fogou at Carn Euny, however, has been fully excavated and is accessible to the public, while the largest known fogou, at Halliggye, Trelowarren, is also in guardianship and open to the public.

History

Written sources prior to the nineteenth century tell us nothing about the history of these villages. Local tradition suggests that Chysauster was occasionally used in the early 1800s for Methodist preachings and was known as the Chapels.

The true nature of the site was not understood until its discovery in 1849 by an antiquary named Crozier. No excavation was attempted until 1873 when the well-known Cornish antiquary William Copeland Borlase cleared out what has since become known as House 6. More work took place in 1897, when two members of the local antiquarian society undertook the excavation of House 4.

No further exploration was done until 1928, when the first major excavation began under the direction of T D Kendrick of the British Museum and Dr Hugh O'Neill Hencken. As a result of this excavation, the owner, Colonel C R R Malone, decided generously to place a large part of the site in the guardianship of the then Office of Works (later the Department of the Environment).

In 1931, Dr Hencken was asked by the Ancient Monuments Inspectorate of the Office of Works to carry out a fuller examination of the site. As a result, Houses 5 and 7 were excavated and further work was done on Houses 3, 4, 6 and 9. In 1936 Colonel Malone placed yet more of his land into guardianship, including Houses 1, 2 and 8, the Fogou and an outlying house to the south-west. All these remain to be examined.

In 1937-39 some repair work and additional excavation took place in Houses 4, 6 and 9, directed by C K Croft Andrew on behalf of the Inspectorate. Since then no further work has been done on the site itself apart from routine maintenance.

In 1984 guardianship of the site passed from the Department of the Environment to English Heritage.

Field System

Chysauster, in common with similar settlements, lies within an extensive field system. The importance of the small fields and trackways associated with early settlements has only been fully appreciated in recent years. At the same time they are fast being eroded by the demands of modern agriculture.

Cornwall has been exceptionally fortunate in retaining much of this complex ancient landscape in the upland areas of the county, but within the last two decades the rate of destruction has increased alarmingly.

During 1983, the field system surrounding the ancient village at

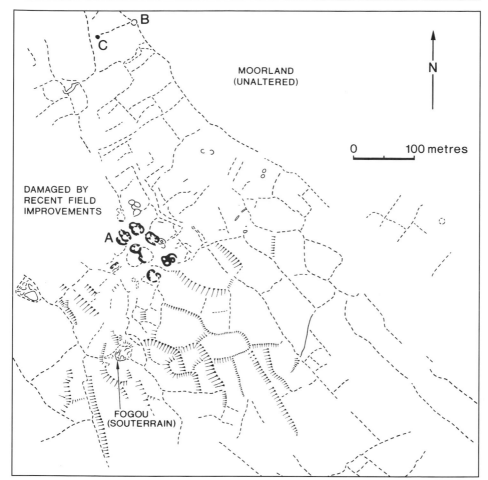

Map of the extensive field systems and trackways at Chysauster. The ancient village is shown at A. Part of an earlier circular house has been excavated at B and a kerbed cairn at C, both of the second millenium BC

Chysauster, which had first been recognised at the time of the 1931 excavations, came under the threat from agricultural improvements. In the winter of 1983/84 salvage work was undertaken : a detailed survey of the entire field system was carried out, supplemented by sample excavation which included the uncovering of a Bronze Age burial cairn incorporated into a later field-wall.

Dating

The courtyard house villages of West Penwith have traditionally been dated to the end of the prehistoric period, that is the later Iron Age, and thought to have continued in use during the Roman period.

They were believed to have been built by people using local hand-made pottery decorated with raised bands or cordons (Cordoned Ware) dated to the first century

Pottery from Chysauster ancient village

BC and first century AD. Recently it has been shown that this type of decoration had a very long life, starting within the local later Iron Age (400BC-43AD) and continuing until the end of the Roman period. So cordons on pots can no longer be used as a satisfactory way of dating.

It is now being seen that where pottery can be associated with courtyard houses, as at Chysauster, it also shows the influence of Roman forms and may conveniently be described as 'Romano-Cornish' ware. As a result, courtyard houses are thought to have been built entirely in the Roman period.

The bulk of the pottery from Chysauster is seen to belong to the second and third centuries AD; pottery from other courtyard-house villages such as Mulfra Vean, Goldherring and Porthmeor belongs to the third and fourth centuries AD. Chysauster then becomes a Romano-Cornish village, contemporary with the later phases at Carn Euny, at which Phase IV, with its courtyard houses, is now thought to start in the second century AD.

The characteristic late Iron Age form of settlement throughout Cornwall, many examples of which have been identified in recent years, is the 'round' – a circular or sub-rectangular earthwork varying in size and containing a varying number of houses within it. This type of enclosed village continued in use, with new ones being built, after the Roman Conquest.

In West Penwith, however, the evidence is less clear. It would seem that courtyard houses of various shapes and sizes became a popular house-form in this furthest tip of the south-western peninsula, while elsewhere in Cornwall oval or boat-shaped houses were built during the Roman period.

It is thought that an earlier phase of settlement must be present on the hillside at Chysauster, as already mentioned. No traces have been found directly beneath the houses so far examined, contrasting with Carn Euny where the new courtyard houses are known to have been built over the Iron Age ones. At Chysauster the earlier settlement could be associated with the fogou to the south and, to judge from some decorated potsherds found in House 7, it may date to the local Iron Age in the last centuries before the Roman Conquest.

Environment and economy

The village lies on a gentle south-western slope between the farms of Chysauster and Carnaquidden in Gulval parish. The granite bedrock is overlain by yellowish brown clay (weathered granite) locally known as rab. The settlement is at the junction of the present agricultural land and the moorland which was, until recently, undisturbed.

Since the excavations were carried out before the days of environmental sampling, there is no direct evidence from the site itself of the crops grown during the life of the settlement. Work on the field system, has, however, produced evidence of cereal cultivation which may tentatively be dated to this period. It has also indicated that the hillside was

Aerial photograph of Chysauster ancient village from the north

originally forested with oak and hazel and that some cultivation may have been practised prior to the building of the Bronze Age cairn.

Information obtained from pollen at other sites in Cornwall suggests that the original woodland cover had already been partly eroded in earlier prehistoric times by the first farmers, so that by the Roman period the uplands would have been cleared of trees and the landscape may have looked much as it does today, with woodland remaining in the valleys.

The acidic conditions which preserve pollen so well inevitably destroy bone and metal objects, and this was certainly the case at Chysauster. No bone is recorded from the excavations, so that we know nothing of the wild and domestic animals that would have lived in and around the village. Equally we know nothing of the metal tools and equipment which must have been used, except that many of them were of iron.

The present boundary of the guardianship area does not enclose the whole of the courtyard house settlement; a further possible courtyard house is shown on the map on page 5 some distance to the south-west. The field systems and evidence of earlier prehistoric occupation are also shown, while the immediate predecessor of the Romano-Cornish settlement may, as already suggested, lie to the south and east in the vicinity of the fogou. Indeed, a mid-nineteenth century account reports that so much of the old village had lately been removed that the fogou no longer lay within it as before. It seems likely that there was once a veritable town on the hillside, of which the houses visible today are the last and latest remnant.

Work in Devon, particularly Exeter, has recently shed more light on the Roman

Grinding corn

conquest of the South West. It would seem that the military occupation west of the Tamar during the second half of the first century AD was short-lived, lasting only 20-25 years. Only one Roman fort has so far been identified in Cornwall, and that was in the north near Wadebridge.

From the second century AD more settled conditions prevailed and trade with the South West increased; certainly Roman goods found their way in considerable quantity to Cornwall, as shown by sites such as Carvossa, near Truro, while the administration of the province had been delegated, perhaps to trusted local chieftains.

Life in the villages would have been little changed from that during pre-conquest years, and was still based on agriculture and stockbreeding. Weaving, grinding corn and other domestic activities were carried out, as shown by the spindle whorls, whetstones and rubbers found.

Spinning

Curiously enough, few querns are recorded from Chysauster, in contrast to the mass of querns of all shapes and sizes found in the excavations at Carn Euny. The nineteenth-century excavations at Chysauster produced part of a rotary quern, but there is no record of any being found in subsequent excavations. It is possible that the stones with a hollow, associated with rubbers, may have served as querns for grinding or pounding certain substances, not necessarily grain. It is interesting to note that comparable stones were found *in situ* at Carn Euny in houses dated to the Romano-Cornish period, suggesting that these 'floor querns' may have become fashionable at this time.

By the third century AD a new factor may have had an impact on the villages and may have brought some local prosperity: the increased demand for Cornish tin. The Iberian mines were in decline. Tin was being increasingly used for coinage and pewter tableware was becoming ever more popular. Chysauster was well-placed, since tin-streaming could have been carried out in the valley to the west, where the remains of extensive modern alluvial tin-workings can be seen. Panning for tin could have become a 'cottage industry' for Romano-Cornish villagers. The fact that only one piece of metallic tin was found during excavations (in House 6) does not preclude such activity, since such a precious commodity would not have been left lying around.

The village appears to have been peacefully abandoned by the end of the Roman period and there is no trace of any later occupation.

The protected site, undisturbed between the agricultural land and the moorland, has become a sanctuary for natural wildlife. It is interesting to note the range of wildflowers and bird-life that can be seen throughout the year.

Ploughing

Description and tour

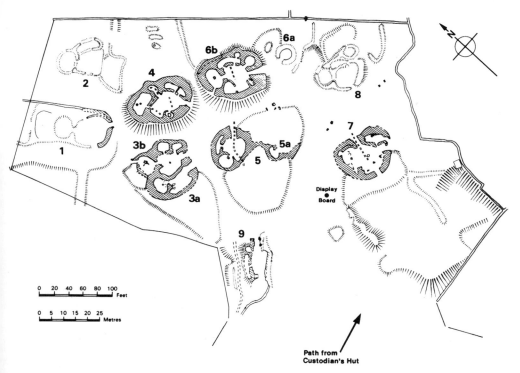

Plan of Chysauster Ancient Village

Visitors are recommended to start their tour of the site by walking up the grass fairway from the custodian's hut, bearing left to reach the first display board. A general idea of the layout of the settlement may be obtained from the site plan. It will be seen that most of the houses are aligned in pairs along a 'street', suggesting an element of planning, in contrast to the apparently haphazard arrangement of the houses at Carn Euny. The Chysauster houses have a number of characteristics in common and these are outlined here so that they may be easily recognised in each house visited.

General Description of the Houses

Each house has a main **Entrance**, which faces away from the prevailing south-west wind. A passage through the thick outer walls leads into an open space, usually 25-30ft (7.6-9m) wide. This space has traditionally been referred to as the **Courtyard** since it was considered to have been unroofed. This may not necessarily have been the case in all courtyard houses, but the term 'courtyard' will be retained for the purpose of this guide.

Left of the entrance, the courtyard in

most cases curves out to form a **Bay** and this would certainly have been comparatively easy to cover with a lean-to roof, forming a shelter or stable for livestock. Opposite the entrance there is a larger, roughly circular room: **the Round Room.** On the right of the entrance is a long narrow room, referred to as the **Long Room** and, in some houses, there is also a small circular room known as the **Small Round Room.**

This general plan is repeated, with minor variations, in every house and suggests that each room had its own special use. Unfortunately the finds from within the houses have been few and it is difficult to relate them to room use. However the fact that the bulk of the finds came in each case from the round room and from the area of the courtyard just outside, suggests that this was the main living room. In contrast, the long rooms and small round rooms produced few finds.

Whether the courtyard was roofed or not, the smaller rooms undoubtedly were, and evidence from other villages indicates that the roofs were of turf or thatch. At Chysauster, however, some of the very small compartments appear to have had stone roofs.

In every round room so far excavated there has been found a **stone with a hollow** in it, commonly believed to have provided the socket for a timber upright supporting the apex of a pyramidal roof. In some houses these stones were also found in the courtyard area. Not all the stones are in their original position, some having been moved by the early excavators. Similar stones with hollows were found during the excavations at Carn Euny and, as mentioned above, recent opinion suggests that some of the Chysauster stones may have been querns. This echoes the interpretation of the first excavator, W C Borlase, who noted the presence of 'mullers' or rubbing-stones in and beside

these 'basins' both at Chysauster and elsewhere.

Certain structural peculiarities of these houses deserve comment: the walls of the entrance passage are invariably exceptionally thick. At the entrance itself the walls are in several cases corbelled inwards towards the top, suggesting preparations for a stone lintel. The rooms or compartments themselves are not so much built as contained within the thickness of the enclosing walls. Evidence from excavation in certain houses suggests that the courtyard may have been paved overall. Stone-robbing for conveniently sized stones over the centuries would account for the absence of paving today. A feature of the house is the **Water Channels**, lined and covered with stone slabs, which were found in the courtyards and some of the small rooms as well.

Finally, visitors will observe that outside almost every house there is a banked and levelled area, referred to as the **Garden Terrace.** Garden plots are known from other courtyard house villages, notably Porthmeor, suggesting that they were a feature of deliberately planned 'new towns' where space was available, in contrast to the urban crowding of Carn Euny, where houses interlock with one another, leaving no room for gardens.

Finds

The bulk of the material excavated from the houses consisted of pottery, as is usual in such settlements. Numerous fragments of slate and a large number of water-worn pebbles, mostly of cream-coloured quartz, were also found. The slate and a few pebbles of greenstone would have been brought to the village from some distance. No satisfactory explanation for the slate and pebbles has been found: Dr Hencken suggested that some of the smaller pebbles could have been sling stones and that the sharp edges and points of freshly broken

House 5, showing the entrance passage leading into the courtyard, with round room beyond

slate may have had some domestic use, since they are not considered to be roofing slates. Other finds included spindle whorls, whetstones, rubbers and several pieces of limonite which may represent the completely rusted remains of iron objects.

Tour of the houses

The houses may be visited in any order. However, since House 5 has the simplest plan and shows these common features most clearly, visitors may wish to see this first. Descriptions of the other houses follow in a clockwise sequence (see site plan on page 10) and end with a note on House 9 to the west and the Fogou to the south. A plan of each excavated house accompanies the text.

House 5

Excavated by Dr H O'Neill Hencken in 1931. The **Entrance Passage** into the **Courtyard** is flanked by big stones on each edge. Notice the two fallen stones at the inner end which may have been door jambs. A stone-lined and covered **Water Channel** ran through the entrance, apparently designed to bring water into the house and then to provide drainage out again under the south-east wall. Some of the stone covers can still be seen in place. These water channels in the courtyards may have related to the possible use of the **Bay** (here clearly seen on the left-hand side of the courtyard) as a cattle stall.

The **Round Room** faces the main entrance, the large blocks of stone which formed its doorway still in place. Also in place as found, just inside the doorway, is a large slab with a small regular hollow, a good example of a **Stone with hollow**. Visitors may like to compare this with those to be seen in most of the other houses. A debris-filled gap found by Dr Hencken in the south-west wall of the round room may possibly have been a 'back door' (see

HOUSE 5

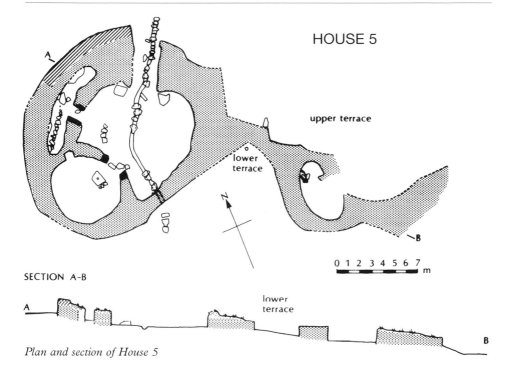

upper terrace

lower terrace

SECTION A-B

A   lower terrace   B

0 1 2 3 4 5 6 7 m

Plan and section of House 5

Houses 3 and 6 where similar gaps exist). The evidence here was not firm, however, and the loose debris has been replaced by modern walling. Standing in the round room one may look south over the lower garden terrace.

On the right of the courtyard, opposite the bay, is the doorway into the **Long Room**, its jambs formed of two large slabs of granite 2ft 10ins (0.86m) high. A large slab found nearby and thought by Dr Hencken to be a possible lintel, would indicate a doorway less then 3ft (0.91m) high, though the walling of the room itself still attained a height of 5ft 6in (1.68m) in places. Similar low doorways appear to have been a common feature of contemporary Cornish buildings. A short section of covered water channel was found in the long room.

Although generally typical in form, House 5 has one unusual feature: this is

The long room of House 5

the thick stone wall which branches away from the east side of the house, acting as a retaining wall for an upper garden terrace. Built into this wall is a small kidney-shaped **Oval Room**, (5a on site plan on page 10) in which Dr Hencken found a hearth with a wide scatter of charcoal and areas of burned floor, indicating continual use. Since no hearth had come to light in the excavation on House 5, he wondered if this 'annexe' might have served as a kitchen. It is also possible that it is all that remains of the round room of another small house. In support of this are the traces of walling and other building activity close by on the 'upper' garden terrace. If this was the case, then House 5 may once have followed the 'semi-detached' layout of nearby House 3.

Close by is House 9, which it may be convenient to visit before House 3 (for details see page 22).

House 3

This lies immediately west of House 5 and was the first to be excavated by Dr Hencken in 1928, further work being done in1931. He noted that the excavations involved the moving of some 50 tons of stone, an indication of the scale of work. Unlike any of the other houses so far excavated, with the possible exception of House 5 above, it takes the form of two 'semi-detached' houses, House 3A to the south and 3B to the north. It is interesting to consider whether they were built together or if one was added to the other. Constructional evidence shows that at the point where the wall of round room 3A meets that of round room 3B, the walls are not bonded together. In fact round room 3B is merely built up against round room 3A, with a vertical break. This implies that round room 3A (and it can be assumed House 3A as a whole) was built first. However Dr Hencken found no evidence to show any great interval between the two, nor that the whole

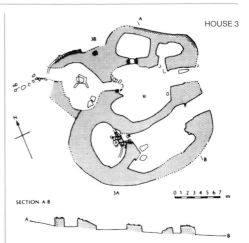

HOUSE 3

SECTION A·B

Plan and section of House 3

structure was not planned and built at one time.

The **Entrances** to both houses are side by side, and face almost due east. It will be seen that **House 3A** consists of an **Entrance Passage, Courtyard** and **Round Room** only; there is no long room. Notice the left door jamb of the round room, still in place and the usual **Stone with Hollow**, also in place; a section of covered **Water Channel** ran between them.

In **House 3B** the partly reconstructed outer entrance leads into an **Entrance Passage** flanked by the usual large stones, still in place. On the south side the excavator found cupmarks, now very indistinct, on one of these stones. Two long stones lie where found and may have been lintels, though the entrance in its present form appears too wide to have been spanned by them. On entering the courtyard, the usual **Bay** is seen on the left; the **Round Room** lies directly ahead, with a well-paved entrance and the left-hand door jamb still in place. A **Stone with hollow** was found in the courtyard but not in its original position. Within the round room, note the paving and curious

Twin entrances of House 3, suggesting a 'semi-detached' arrangement

stone structure at first thought to be a hearth. Excavation revealed no signs of charcoal or burning, however, and its purpose remains obscure. It may have been built or altered in historic times, possibly as a platform at the time of the Methodist 'preachings'. The 'back door' seen in this room was not particularly convincing and may well be due to later wall damage. A covered **Water Channel** outside on the north was probably designed to divert surface water from the walls of the round room.

On the north side of the courtyard the usual long room at first appears to have been converted into two **Small Round Rooms**. However, the dividing wall, the two good doorways and the step up into the left-hand room seem to have been part of the original structure, so these rooms may have been planned to replace a long room from the start. A triangular **Garden Terrace** runs from the walls of House 3A towards the south and there is a small terrace outside the round room of House 3B.

Before leaving House 3 the visitor may like to consider the proposition that, when 3B was added, its courtyard bay may have replaced a previously-built long room in House 3A. Against this, no evidence was found of a blocked long room entrance in what became the dividing wall. A complete rebuilding of this wall, including the removal of door jambs and lintel, is of course possible. The sequence of planning and building of this house thus remains an interesting puzzle.

House 1

This site, immediately north-west of House 3, is only partly cleared and has not been excavated. However the general outline is recognisable as a house, though the stone hedge running in from the north-west partly overlies the original house-wall on the north. The cleared east wall can be seen, curving round to the entrance, with its two door jamb stones in place. Inside, the outline of a **Courtyard** and **Round**

Room can be traced. A **Garden Terrace** lies to the south.

House 2

Immediately to the north-east of House 1 the low outlines of House 2 can be seen, also unexcavated and only superficially cleared. By referring to the site plan on page 10, the usual layout of a **Courtyard, Round Room** and **Long Room** can just be distinguished, with a **Garden Terrace** to the south and east.

House 4

Immediately to the north of House 3 lies House 4, excavated by Cornish and Holman, two members of the Penzance Natural History and Antiquarian Society, in 1897. Like House 6 next to it, it was built on an artificial platform of earth and stones, banked up on the south to counteract the slope of the hill. After excavation, its condition then deteriorated for over 30 years, until Chysauster was taken into guardianship. Following preliminary clearing and consolidation work in 1928 and 1931 under Dr Hencken, further excavation of the interior and repair

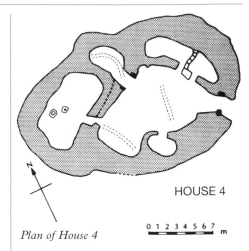

HOUSE 4

0 1 2 3 4 5 6 7 m

Plan of House 4

work were undertaken by the Ministry of Works in 1938 under the direction of C K Croft Andrew.

The **Entrance Passage** is unusual, being shaped a little like an hour-glass. Note the fine paving of the entrance extending into the 'street'. Continuing into the **Courtyard**, the visitor will see the usual **Bay** on the left with a covered **Water Channel** running across it. To the left of the bay is a small room which seems to be

Paved entrance passage of House 4, leading into the courtyard

Courtyard of House 4 with, on the left, a covered water channel

Round room of House 4 with, in the left foreground, a stone with hollow

original though its shape has been modified by exposure and repair. The excavators did not record any evidence to suggest its use, but it may have served the same purpose as a similar small chamber in House 6 which appears to be a sump for the storage of rainwater (see page18).

The wall between the courtyard and the **Round Room** has been much disturbed and reconstructed. Note, however, the fine paving and the usual **Stone with hollow**, though it may not be any longer in its original place, and the stone-lined pit.

The stonework of the **Long Room** has also suffered a great deal of deterioration and subsequent reconstruction. It may have been divided into two at some stage, with a second entrance beside the original doorway, but the evidence for this is not now clear. The interior walls of the **Small Round Room** next to it have also been considerably modified though the two big stones forming the door jambs are still in place. Note the covered **Water Channel** running out into the courtyard and another small stone-lined pit.

House 6

This lies south-east of House 4 and was excavated by Borlase in 1873. Like House 4, it had seriously deteriorated by the time Hencken started work in 1928. He found time to clear the exterior and to examine and strengthen the walls, noting that some of them appeared to have been reconstructed and heightened in relatively recent times. House 6 was further re-examined in 1937-38 by C K Croft

Andrew who carried out some quiet extensive excavation which has never been published. Like House 4, this house was built on a specially constructed platform, banked up from the south to make a level site. Its layout appears to be more elaborate than the other houses so far excavated.

The long **Entrance Passage** now narrows towards the inner end, but the original line of the walls is not certain owing to subsequent modification and reconstruction. The passage leads into the **Courtyard** and the usual **Bay** will be seen on the left. The **Stone with hollow** is not in its original position.

Immediately inside the courtyard, on the left, notice the unusual **Small Chamber**. Its construction, with the dividing wall bonded into the main outer wall, shows that it was part of the original plan. Excavation revealed a **Sump** sunk in the floor against the outer wall, with provision for overflow through the wall. Several **Water Channels** were found to run towards this sump from the courtyard. Because of damage the connection to the

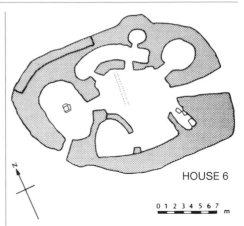

HOUSE 6

0 1 2 3 4 5 6 7 m

Plan of House 6

sump was not complete, but it seems likely that it was intended to store rain water. A raised platform found along the left-hand side of this little chamber may have provided a convenient access for dipping water. As with House 4, this supply system may have been an alternative to the water channels running through house entrances found in Houses 5 and 7, here made

Courtyard of House 6, showing on the right the entrance and a covered water channel, and on the left the small round room with paving at a higher level

Detailed view of House 6, with on the left the courtyard and covered water channel. At the centre of the photograph is a stone with a hollow. In the right foreground can be seen the long room with a stone room-divider. In the centre background is the round room

impossible by the slope of the ground. Hencken found a small **Stone with hollow** at the entrance to this room, but it was upside down, so its original position is unknown. During the 1873 excavations, Borlase noted some evidence which suggested that this small chamber had been roofed with stone.

The **Round Room**, as usual directly across the courtyard from the entrance, suffered considerable reconstruction by Borlase. Hencken's examination showed that the south wall may have been rebuilt on the wrong line. Excavation revealed a horseshoe-shaped platform round the north side of the room, thought possibly to have been used as a sleeping bench. The flat, upright stone, still in place, marks a hearth area. The usual **Stone with hollow** was

found, but is not in place. The '**back door**' is original and was discovered by Croft Andrew in 1937.

The slightly raised **Long Room** is unusual and presents an interesting problem. The two good entrances, both of which appear to be original, suggest that the intention was to construct two rooms with a dividing wall (compare the two small rooms in House 3B). However, the stones that remain in place, which are not structural, suggest a 'room-divider' rather than a permanent partition. A section of covered water channel and pit were found by Croft Andrew in the left-hand section of this room. In the right-hand section the small **Circular chamber** recessed into the outside wall may have been used for storage, the raised floor perhaps intended

Circular chamber in exterior wall of House 6, viewed from the entrance of the long room

to keep its contents dry. Note the **Corbel stones** discovered by Borlase and still in place, indicating that this small chamber was originally roofed with stone.

Between the long room and the entrance passage is a **Small Round Room** with paved floor, on a considerably higher level than the courtyard. Remains of a fire and pottery were found by Borlase in this room.

Outside the walls of House 6 is a roughly **circular structure** showing traces of stone facing. Since its entrance faces towards House 6, its seems likely to relate to this house, and may have been an annexe (Shown as 6A on site plan between House 6 and House 8). There is a large **Garden Terrace** relating to House 6, extending uphill to the north.

House 8

This lies south-east of House 6 and although, like House 1 and House 2, it has not been excavated, its plan is reasonably clear. The remains of a **Courtyard, Round Room, Long Room** and **Small Round Room** can all be traced. There is

a small **Garden Terrace** to the north, part of a larger terraced area enclosed by a low bank.

House 7

South-west of House 8 is House 7, excavated by Dr Hencken in 1931. He found it very badly ruined, with little internal wall-facing remaining. There were also signs of considerable alterations and the original plan was much more difficult to trace than in other houses excavated. The cause of this degree of destruction, unusual at Chysauster though more evident at Carn Euny, may be stone-robbing: a number of relatively modern stone hedges run nearby. Some clearing and rebuilding may also have been done at the time of the Methodist 'preachings'. The tenant at Chysauster farm in 1931 told Dr Hencken he remembered being taken to hear a sermon in the ruins of the house in 1862. The two antiquaries, Edmonds (1861) and Blight (1855), mentioned recent damage to the village in this area.

The entrance to House 7 raises an interesting problem. There was at one time

HOUSE 7

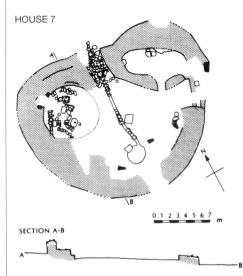

SECTION A-B

Plan and section of House 7

House 7, showing on the left the original entrance and on the right the long room.

an **Entrance Passage** in the normal position on the east side. Note the large upright stone similar to other 'door jambs' still in place in the outer wall at this point, and the large stone lying outside which may have been the opposite jamb stone. This entrance was at some time blocked with rough stone walling. However both the **Long Room** and the **Bay** in the courtyard are in the usual position in relation to this entrance (now unblocked). The paved entrance on the north can certainly be shown to be ancient also, and the fact that there is the usual **Water Channel** running in through it, connected to a sump found in the courtyard, suggest that it, too, may have been part of the original house. Its unusual position on the north and the blocking of the east entrance implies that the house was modified at some point during its occupation and this entrance added at that time. To make matters even more complicated there appears to be a third entrance on the south side. However Dr Hencken traced modern cart or sledge ruts running through this gap, across the courtyard and over the water channel in the paved entrance and came to the conclusion that this breach in the wall was quite recent.

The remains of the **Round Room** are to be seen in the usual place opposite the east entrance, which again tends to confirm this as the 'planned' entrance. Notice the stone paving and the **Stone with hollow** ('a' on the plan) still in place. The remains of two hearths ('b' and 'c' on the plan) were found in this room, and a short section of covered **Water Channel**. The recess in the wall between two large jamb stones is thought to be original, but it has also been suggested that it served as a pulpit for Methodist preachers and may have been partly rebuilt. The modern cart-gap entrance leads out to the south on to a small **Garden Terrace**. Beyond this is a

House 7, showing the later entrance, and a modern breach in the wall beyond

further banked and terraced area.

House 9

This house, close to the western site boundary, appears to be on a smaller scale than the other houses, but this may be partly due to the intrusive modern stone hedge. It was partly excavated in 1931 and further clearance and excavation were carried out in 1938–39.

The house differs from most of the others in the village in having its main axis north and south instead of east and west, but what remains of its plan conforms to the usual layout. An **Entrance Passage** from the north leads into the **Courtyard** with the **Bay** on the left. On the right are the **Long Room** and a **Small Round Room** – the only one in the village to contain a **Hearth**. One jamb stone of the doorway into the round room survives, but the rest of this room seems to have been destroyed in the building of the stone hedge, which overlies the position of the east wall in the room, and of the main east wall of the house.

Fogou

Before leaving Chysauster the visitor is recommended to see the Fogou, but should note that, at the time of writing, only the exterior may be viewed for reasons of safety. The fogou lies about 135 yards (123m) south-east of House 7, close to the southern site boundary. It was partially excavated by Borlase, who found its floor to be some 6ft (1.9m) below existing ground level. Many of the massive capstones had

Hearth in the small round room of House 9

been removed but two remain in position and another has fallen. (The blocking of the present entrance is a temporary safety measure.)

It is interesting to note that in 1861 Richard Edmonds reported that the stone-lined underground structure then ran up the hill for at least 50ft. He added that so much of the village had recently been removed that the fogou, once within the village, now lay outside it, thus confirming that the settlement was once much larger than it appears today.

Note: Much better preserved and more impressive fogous are to be seen at Carn Euny (see page 35) and at Halliggye on the Lizard, which is also in guardianship.

Carn Euny

Introduction

Carn Euny is a village of the Iron Age and Romano-British period, established before 400 BC and occupied into the fourth century AD. It is especially notable for the well-preserved souterrain, locally known as a 'fogou', which lies centrally within the village and is unique in plan. This ancient village, formerly known as Chapel Euny, lies on a south-west slope just above the 500ft (152m) contour, on granite uplands rich in antiquities. The hill above the village is crowned by the circular Iron Age fort of Caer Brane. Across the dry valley to the north-west rises the mass of Bartinney Downs, also with a prehistoric enclosure on its summit, while in the valley below the site near the hamlet of Brane is a small, well-preserved entrance grave and other evidence of prehistoric activity. To the south-east, about one mile away, is Gold-herring, a village dating from the first few centuries AD, excavated by the Cornwall

House I and the entrance to the fogou

Archaeological Society 1958-61.

Immediately above the site to the north-west are the remains of a settlement and field system. These lie on the south-facing slopes of Bartinney Downs, near the holy well and chapel (destroyed) of St Uny from which the site derives its name. Six freestanding round houses have been identified at the northern end of what was once an extensive rectilinear field system. The houses and fields, which together cover some 24 hectares, are thought to date from Bronze Age and Iron Age times and presumably the lower part developed into the village of Carn Euny during the second half of the first millennium BC.

Nothing appears to have been known of the fogou or settlement at Carn Euny before the first half of the nineteenth century, when it was discovered by miners prospecting for tin. The land at this time was owned by the Rashleigh family of Menabilly. Between 1863 and 1868 the Cornish antiquary William Copeland Borlase carried out excavations in the fogou and presented the results to the Society of Antiquaries of London. He does not appear to have excavated the settlement, however, and it was not until the 1920s that any houses were examined, when House I and House II were partially excavated by local residents, Dr Favell and Canon Taylor.

In 1953 the site was taken into guardianship by the former Ministry of Works and cleared of its covering of gorse and brambles. Between 1964 and 1972 an extensive series of excavations was carried out, with the dual aim of examining the fogou prior to repair and conservation of the structure, and of revealing a more intelligible plan of the settlement for display to the public. Excavation of the fogou, inside and out, has produced some interesting information, not least that the monument was built in several stages.

The Settlement

The village which surrounds the fogou has suffered from much rebuilding and stone-robbing which accounts for its present ruined appearance. Clearance for small plot cultivation in recent times had added to this process of denudation.

On the west of this site a small rectangular cottage had been built over earlier occupation. The pottery found within the cottage dates from the mid-eighteenth century to around 1800 and by the mid-nineteenth century it had already fallen into disuse.

Excavation of the settlement has provided information on the houses and equipment of the later Iron Age (400 BC–AD 43) and the Roman period, supplementing that already obtained from other excavated villages in the region such as Chysauster (also in guardianship), Porthmeor near Zennor and neighbouring Goldherring. These settlements all contain a compartmented house-form peculiar to west Cornwall, but not unlike other cellular houses known from Wales and elsewhere in the highland zone of Britain. These 'courtyard house' villages, as they are known in Cornwall, are confined to the Land's End peninsula where they are all, with few exceptions, situated between 350ft (106m) and 600ft (189m) above sea level.

A recent survey has recorded 40 sites, of which 21 are established, 10 are possible and 9 have been destroyed. So far only one courtyard house is known from the Isles of Scilly, on Halangy Down, St Mary's.

A **courtyard house** is usually oval, enclosed by an immensely thick outer wall faced inside and out with dry stone masonry and with massive foundation stones or 'grounders'. A paved entrance facing away from the prevailing south-west winds leads into a 'courtyard' off which open small rooms built within the thickness of the enclosing wall. A large oval or circular room

Carn Euny Ancient Village: a reconstruction showing an oval stone house (House III)

opposite the entrance is thought to be the main living room, with one or more long narrow rooms and recesses on either side of the courtyard serving various functions such as storage and stabling. Stone-capped drains for bringing water both in and out of the houses are a feature. (Similar drains can be seen in the older Cornish farmyards today.) Thatch roofing is thought to have covered the rooms, leaving the courtyard open to the sky, though this is not certain and the roofing may have covered the courtyard area as well. The pottery from these houses indicates that they were built in the Roman period, mostly during the second and third centuries AD.

As well as the compartmented houses, these villages contain oval houses of simpler design. There are three surviving examples at Carn Euny and the best of these, House A, is the standard house-type for the whole of Cornwall at this time.

In some cases, and Carn Euny is a good

example, these courtyard house villages were built over earlier settlements dating to the later Iron Age (400 BC–AD 43).

Fogou

A 'fogou' named after a late Cornish word meaning 'cave', is an underground or partly underground structure. The fine underground structure at Carn Euny is unique in having a round chamber as well as the long passage characteristic of most fogous. Cornish fogous belong to a group of monuments variously described as souterrains and 'earth houses' known from other parts of Britain and Ireland, some of which date from the Iron Age but which also continued to be built during and after the Roman period. In Ireland, ogham stones have been found incorporated into some examples, showing that they were still being built in the early Christian era.

Cornish fogous are partly or wholly subterranean, built in large trenches,

Carn Euny Ancient Village: a reconstruction of a timber house (House A1 described on page 41)

though some above-ground examples exist. They consist of a main passage, often aligned east to west or north-east to south-west. This passage is built of dry-stone walling, corbelled inwards, and roofed with massive capstones. Subsidiary chambers and small narrow side passages ('creeps') are a feature of the structures. Fogous are found only in the extreme west of Cornwall, mainly in the Land's End peninsula and round the Fal estuary. All known examples are associated with the remains of settlements, some of which were fortified.

Most fogous provide evidence of being built during the later Iron Age (400 BC–AD 43).

There has been no lack of theories as to the original function of fogous, from hide-outs in time of trouble, to cellars for storing goods and livestock. The 'cellar' interpretation is the one favoured by some scholars. At Carn Euny, however, excavations suggest that some souterrains at least may have been non-utilitarian, and could have been built for religious purposes, recalling the 'parish church' of historic times. The Round Chamber at Carn Euny is particularly interesting, since it appears that there may have been an earlier cult centre here before the Long Passage was ever built.

Dating

At Carn Euny, and some other 'courtyard house' sites, there is evidence of occupation before the Iron Age and Roman periods. A few Mesolithic flints as well as Neolithic and Bronze Age finds from the excavations and from the immediate vicinity point to sporadic activity in earlier prehistoric times. However the first trace of actual settlement on the site itself dates from the fifth century BC and the occupation appears to have been more or less continuous from then until the fourth century AD – a period of over 700 years.

Four main phases of occupation (see Chronological Chart) have been distinguished at Carn Euny, as a result of the excavations by the Department of the Environment and more recent studies of the pottery, particularly from other Cornish sites belonging to the Roman period. The earliest phase (Phase I) starts

Chronological chart

Phase	Date	Buildings	Artefacts
I	About 500BC to 300BC	Fogou : round chamber and (later) long passage. ?Timber and turf houses.	Stamp-decorated pottery, nearly all of local granitic clay.
II	About 300BC to 50BC	Timber and turf houses of House A1 type.	Roulette-decorated pottery, jars with tooled curvilinear decoration and early cordoned pots (South-western Decorated Ware). Granitic clay still in use, but some pots now of gabbroic clay imported from the Lizard peninsula. Querns. Spindlewhorls of stone and pot.
III	About 50BC to AD100	Stone and earlier timber houses in use.	Cordoned Ware jars and bowls. Undecorated pots of gabbroic clay. Spindelwhorls (some re-used potsherds). Querns, iron brooch and pruning hook.
IV	Second to fourth centuries AD	Courtyard houses built; also oval stone houses of House A type. ?Fogou opened at east end.	Romano-British pottery and fragments of Samian Ware. Roman glass beads. Spindlewhorls and rotary querns.

Sometime before AD400 the site became abandoned.

Mid-eighteenth century AD : cottage built of west side.

Pottery from Phases I to IV, drawn by reconstruction from fragments found during the excavations

in the fifth century BC or earlier and continues into the fourth. The second phase (Phase II) is thought to span the third and second centuries BC, continuing into the mid-first century BC. Traces of this earlier settlement, with pottery of South-Western Decorated type and timber-built houses, owe their survival to the later courtyard house settlement being built on top. Phase III, which saw the introduction of local pottery decorated with raised bands or cordons (Cordoned Ware) starts around 50 BC and lasts through the first century AD, merging with the latest phase (Phase IV) when native pottery influenced by Roman wares was being made and courtyard houses were being built. Phase IV spans the second, third and part of the fourth centuries of our era, coinciding with the second phase at nearby Goldherring and with other courtyard-house villages in West Penwith. It is the stone houses from this last phase which are visible today.

The village ceased to be occupied some time during the fourth century and the absence of any medieval pottery suggests that it was abandoned for several centuries.

Post-medieval pottery was found in the cottage and elsewhere on the site, particularly in House I where it may have been associated with later activity in the fogou. (In the 1860s Borlase found the long passage completely filled up with earth, while the east entrance had been deliberately blocked by a large boulder and other carefully placed stones.)

Environmental background

The village lies on sloping ground with rab (decayed granite) subsoil overlying the coarse-grained granite which forms the bed-rock of the Land's End peninsula. Rab mainly consists of yellowish brown clay produced as the result of the solid granite becoming altered under soil-forming conditions. It can achieve considerable thicknesses, and here it is at least 6ft (2m) thick, though higher up the slope the thickness decreases. Near the top of the hill the granite outcrops at the surface where the remains of a quarry can be seen.

Wherever the moor has not been cultivated, granite boulders ('moorstone') abound and these would have provided a ready source of building material at all periods. Once the village had been built, however, an even better source of conveniently sized stone was provided by the houses themselves during periods of rebuilding, while the village has been used as a 'quarry' by the local inhabitants until recent times. The rab was extensively used by the early builders (as modern builders might use cement) for floors, packing round posts, and in the walls. In addition to rab, kaolinized granite (China clay) occurs locally and was used as floor materials in the houses.

The settlement lies almost at the limit of the present agricultural land, beyond which is the moor with its typical flora of gorse, heaths and grasses. Bushes and a few stunted trees are all that can be seen today, growing around scattered farmsteads or natural granite outcrops. However pollen was well preserved in the acidic soil on the site and analysis of this has provided some interesting information. It appears that the landscape was not always so denuded of trees and that extensive deciduous woodland once existed on these uplands. Man's inroads into this forest may have already started before the Bronze Age, but increased with the extension of arable farming practised by the inhabitants of Carn Euny and neighbouring settlements during the later Bronze Age and Iron Age. Certainly at the time the fogou was built, probably starting in the fifth century BC, there were more trees, including oak, than during the later phases of the settlement, when considerable clearance for fields must have been made.

The conditions which preserve pollen so well inevitably destroy bone and metal objects. As a result, the environmental and economic picture is incomplete and we know little or nothing of the wild and domestic animals which were undoubtedly present. Equally we know little of the tools and equipment made of metal which must have been used by the villagers.

The present boundary of the village does not enclose the whole of the settlement, which is believed to extend further west and south and may originally have been of the unenclosed type. The boundary on the east, and possibly the north, could be an early wall, at least in its lower part, associated with the later phases of the settlement. Traces of an earlier field system can, in certain conditions, be distinguished in the field immediately east of the site, but ploughing is fast obliterating these lynchets. Other fields to the north and west, on the slopes of Bartinney Downs, have already been mentioned and could have been farmed in all the phases of occupation. Carn Euny therefore, like other similar settlements in West Penwith such as

Chysauster, lies within an extensive field system of great antiquity, with origins in the Bronze Age or earlier.

Economy

The Celtic inhabitants of Carn Euny were certainly farmers and probably traders. They may have dealt in tin (cassiterite pebbles have been found in the excavations and it is known that tin was streamed in the valley below in historic times). As farmers and stockbreeders, they would have worked some 40 acres (16ha) or more of arable land around the village. Cereal pollen has been found and oats, barley and rye, which were all recorded from Goldherring, could have been grown as well as wheat. Although nothing is known of the domestic animals kept by the villagers, small fragments of bone from the excavations indicate the presence of sheep or goats and probably cattle. Pigs and other livestock as well as various wild animals and birds would have supplemented the diet and provided useful raw materials. Weaving, grinding corn and other domestic industries were carried out. Querns of various types, whetstones, rubbers and mauls, also spindlewhorls of stone and pottery, have been found in all phases of the settlement.

Apart from stone and pottery, little has

Saddle and rotary quernstones, whetstone and worked stone disc found during the excavations

Iron pruning-hook, brooch, stone spindle whorl and glass beads found during the excavations

survived from the Iron Age and Romano-British period owing partly to the destructive action of the acid soil on anything of bone or metal, but also perhaps due to improved manuring techniques introduced during the Roman period whereby domestic debris was regularly removed and used as fertilizer. In the few cases where such middens or dumps have survived on Cornish sites of this time, a wealth of objects has been found which includes metalwork, glass and imported pottery. However, two iron objects – a pruning hook and a brooch – have survived at Carn Euny by virtue of being buried in rab which is rather less corrosive than the humic soil.

An amphora fragment dated to the first century BC shows that that Cornwall was in contact with the Roman world well before the Roman conquest, either directly across the Channel or via British trading posts up the coast such as Mount Batten (Plymouth) or Hengistbury and Cleavel Point (Poole Harbour) in Dorset. The main Roman influence appears to have been during the second-fourth centuries AD, just when courtyard houses became fashionable, and this may have been connected with the increasing demand for Cornish tin by the third century. In most ways, however, the inhabitants of West Penwith seem to have been little affected by their conquerors and the same pattern of life, enhanced by new house styles and some imported Roman luxuries, continued at Carn Euny until late Roman times. After the fourth century AD the village seems to have been abandoned for more than a thousand years.

Description and Tour

General description of the houses

The village has suffered extensive damage over the years through stone robbing for field walls, gate posts, stock shelters and other structures, and by the cultivation of plots for daffodils or potatoes. Miners prospecting for tin in the early nineteenth century caused considerable damage to the fogou as well as the settlement. As a result, the original form of the houses, particularly the large ones of courtyard house type, is far from clear.

More than ten houses belonging to the Iron Age and Romano-British occupation have been excavated. Three are large enclosures (House I, House II and House IV) with internal north-south diameters of more than 40ft (12m) and the remainder are smaller, mostly oval enclosures more akin to the oval houses common in the rest of Cornwall during the Roman period. The stone houses visible today date from the last phase of the village.

The apparently haphazard arrangement of the houses at Carn Euny is in contrast to Chysauster, where the houses are set on each side of a street, but it does occur at other courtyard-house villages. Indeed recent surveys have shown that the regularity of Chysauster is exceptional and a more haphazard arrangement is found at most villages. At Carn Euny the building of houses on top of the earlier village and around the fogou would have caused the irregular layout.

The pattern of interlocking houses seen at Carn Euny compares with that at the fine courtyard-house site of Bossullow Trehyllys (Madron) and with the guardianship site of Halangy Down on St Mary's, Isles of Scilly, where a series of similar interlocking structures is broadly contemporary with the later phases at Carn Euny.

Building methods changed little during the Iron Age in the South West, though some of the early round houses at Carn Euny may have had turf or wattle walls as well as stone. These have completely disappeared and only the semi-circular drainage gullies running round the uphill part of such houses inside the since-vanished walls indicated their existence. Pits for posts, packed with rab and stones, survived in houses of all periods, showing that timber was extensively used throughout. With the continuing clearance of woodland, however, trees suitable for structural timber must have become increasingly scarce towards the end of the settlement.

It is not known for certain how the houses were roofed. The Iron Age round houses probably had conical roofs of thatch supported on timber posts and the reconstruction drawing of House A1 on page 26 shows how they may have looked. The oval stone houses of the Roman period are less easy to reconstruct but an attempt has been made with House III on page 25, while a drawing of well-preserved courtyard houses at Chysauster can be seen on page 3.

The numbers and letters of the houses shown on the site plan relate to the order in which they were excavated, and have no chronological significance. They can therefore be visited in any order, but the route described below may be found helpful.

Start from the entrance, walk up the hill on the eastern side and enter Courtyard

House II on the left (see site plan).

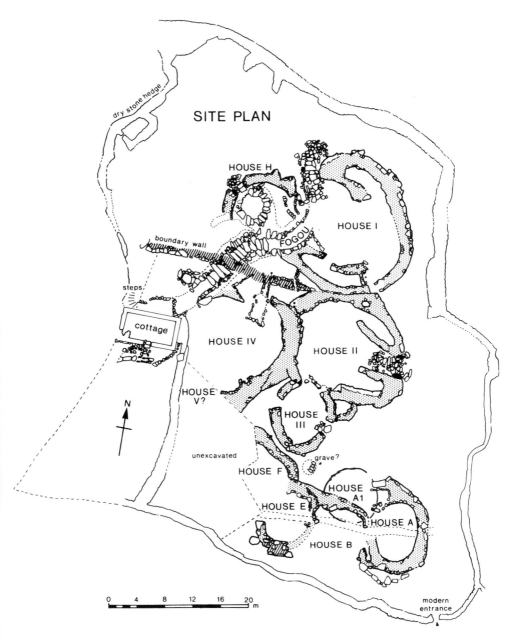

SITE PLAN

dry stone hedge

HOUSE H

HOUSE I

FOGOU

boundary wall

steps

cottage

HOUSE IV

HOUSE II

HOUSE
V?

HOUSE
III

unexcavated

grave?

HOUSE F

HOUSE
A1

HOUSE E

HOUSE A

HOUSE B

modern
entrance

N

0   4   8   12   16   20
                        m

Plan of Carn Euny Ancient Village

House II

HOUSE II

This large irregular enclosure of courtyard-house type is approached through a fine paved entrance, flanked by two well-defined rooms, both of which had been previously examined. In the case of Room 1 on the north, nothing remained over the floor, which had been previously excavated to the rab subsoil. Note the alcove, possibly a cupboard, in the north wall and a blocked opening in the south wall. In Room 2 (which may not be an original feature of the courtyard house) pits and gullies belonging to timber structures of earlier phases of the village were found, often covered by layers of rab deliberately relaid.

Later cultivation had removed most of the Iron Age features from the courtyard but a drain flowing across the enclosure and out through the main entrance was found, as well as traces of further gullies and pits. Two good postholes found in the main entrance on the east may have held

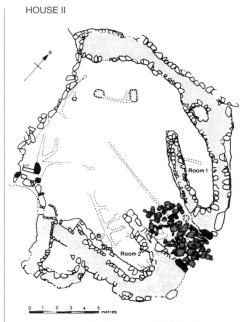

Plan of House II. Note the well-defined rooms each side of the entrance

The entrance of House II, showing the paving and the large courtyard beyond

House I, the paved entrance in the foreground and the fogou to the right

posts for a wooden gate. On the south-west, paving and a narrow 'entrance' appear to connect this house with House III. The enclosure wall interlocks with other houses on all sides except the east, where the settlement is thought to have been bounded by a roadway.

In common with other large enclosures of courtyard-house type, as well as the smaller houses, both here and elsewhere in the region, House II would have been wholly or partly covered by a roof, though we cannot be sure of the exact form this would have taken.

On leaving House II by the main east entrance, turn left up the hill once again and pass round the outside of House I. Note the stone-built drain emerging here at the base of the wall. Continuing round the outside of the House I wall, a fine paved entrance is reached which leads into the house and also gives access to the fogou on the right.

House I

This is the best preserved of the large enclosures, with evidence for two rooms (Room 1 on the north, Room 2 on the south) contemporary with the main oval enclosure. Much modification and rebuilding took place over the years, however, and the remains of a later wall of large stones built inside the house wall can be seen on the east side: it was probably built to widen and heighten the original wall. Cultivation of the interior has since destroyed most of the internal features. Gullies, pits and post-holes belonging to

HOUSE I

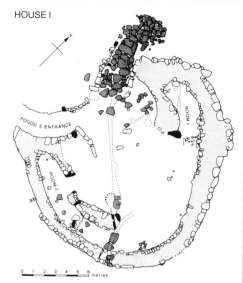

Plan of House I

the earlier phases of occupation were preserved under the courtyard house wall on the east and south, as well as under the entrance. A drain flowed under the entrance paving and down into the enclosure, in a gully cut through the rab, to a pit filled with a large boulder. Three drain lids cover the eastern part of the pit, where the gully passed through. It then continued past the end of Room 2, from where a stone-lined culvert carried the water out through an opening in the south wall of the house, already seen from the outside.

Although House I has some features which can be compared with Houses 5 and 7 at Chysauster, its proximity to the fogou and the opening up of the latter in Phase IV, must have dictated the plan above all else. The enclosure is clearly connected with the fogou and it is possible that a covered way led down the paved entrance passage from a roadway round the north and east of the site. Beneath this entrance were found pits and a trench dating from the earliest phase of the settlement. Charcoal found in this trench has given a radiocarbon date in the fifth century BC.

Fogou

After its discovery early in the nineteenth

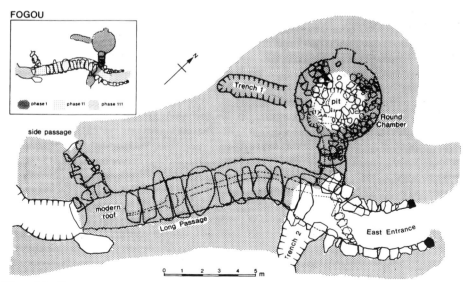

Plan of the Fogou

Looking south-west along the fogou passage

century, the fogou was excavated and surveyed between 1862 and 1867 by W C Borlase and J R Blight. Little change has taken place since then, and the main features shown on this nineteenth-century survey were confined by the present excavations. The structure consists of the following elements : (1) an unroofed sloping *east entrance* which provides access today; (2) a *long curved passage* with eleven capstones in their original positions and a *side passage* ('creep') leading to the surface near the south-west end; (3) *a round corbelled chamber* and *integral entrance passage*, roofed with four capstones, opening off the long passage. Excavation has shown that these three groups represent three main building phases, which may equate with phases of the settlement. In

this case, the round chamber and its entrance passage would belong to Phase I. The long passage, in which was found a distinctive type of decorated pottery now known as 'Carn Euny Ware' (see page 27) would belong to Phases II and III, and the sloping east entrance to Phase IV.

The plan of the fogou shows the structure as it is today, with two capstones replaced at the south-west end and a concrete roof between them to consolidate the passage walls. The other eleven capstones of the long passage and the four capstones of the entrance passage to the round chamber remained as they were in the nineteenth century, with the exception of the first capstone at the east end which had tilted out of position (no doubt due to miners who appear to have blasted their

The interior of the covered chamber of the fogou

way in here) and was righted during excavations.

From within House I, the fogou is approached down the sloping *East Entrance*. Two uprights mark the end of the passage walling where it opens into House I. The straight joint in the north wall further down on the right indicates the point where the original passage is thought to have ended, up against the natural rab, before the present entrance was made. At the base of the slope, after the large stone on end partly blocking the passage, is the entrance to the round chamber. Beyond this the roofing of the main passage begins, though at least three further capstones to the east would have been present originally. Note the opening in the south wall of the passage here, giving on to a shallow trench outside (Trench 2 on plan of fogou).

The Round Corbelled Chamber is reached through a low *Entrance Passage* which may have extended further south-east (Trench 2 on plan) before being cut by the long passage. The round chamber was paved with flat stone slabs and remains of this paving are still visible. A pit in the centre (see plan) may have been an original Iron Age feature and could have held a roof support. The walls consist of interlocking rings of dry-stone masonry constructed within a large pit, dug through the rab to a depth of 8ft (2.4m) at its deepest (uphill) part. The section drawing shows how the masonry is corbelled inward to give the top course a diameter of 10–11ft (3–3.35m) whereas the base diameter is 15ft (4.6m).

Section

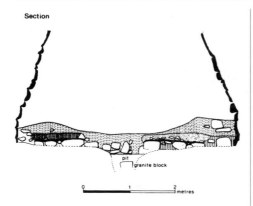

pit
granite block

0   1   2 metres

Elevation

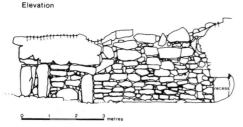

recess

0   1   2   3 metres

Section (top) and elevation of the corbelled round chamber of the fogou

Note the *recess* in the wall opposite the entrance. Excavation has confirmed that relatively soft natural rab forms the back of the recess today, though a backing in stone or some other material would almost certainly have existed originally.

Excavation outside the chamber on the west uncovered a deep, slightly curving *construction trench* (Trench 1 on plan). It was cut down through the natural rab level with the bottom of the pit for the round chamber, into which it had originally opened. The building of the stone lining of the chamber effectively sealed the opening so that no indication of the trench's presence is suspected today from the inside. The discovery of this trench allowed the back of the chamber wall to be examined in this small area. As can be seen in the section drawing along Trench 1, the corbelling technique used increasingly

large and long stones for each rising course, so that the back of the stones forms a near-vertical face, while the upper course has an overhang of 2½–3ft (0.75–0.9m). The chamber is therefore a potentially free-standing structure of interlocking rings and, in view of the size of blocks in the surviving upper course, which is already 8ft (2.4m) above the excavated floor, it is unlikely that the roof could ever have been completed by a stone dome, as had been suggested before the excavation. It must therefore have been either open to the sky, or roofed with timber and thatch (or turf) around a central post. (The chamber has recently been roofed by English Heritage for safety reasons).

Returning through the low doorway of the entrance passage, carefully built of uprights and lintel in typical Iron Age fashion, turn right down the fine curved *Long Passage* of the fogou. Owing to the slope of the land, the passage is only partially underground; it measures 66ft (20.1m) long, excluding the sloping east end down which the fogou is entered. The dry-stone walls are corbelled inwards and built in a trench dug through the rab. The upper courses and roof are just proud of the ground surface and were originally covered by a slight mound of earth and rab, retained on the south side by a wall of vertical slabs. (Part of this revetment wall can be seen on the outside when visiting the area north of House IV.) The passage is 6ft 6in (2m) wide at the base and 6ft (1.8m) high throughout most of its length, diminishing toward the south-west end. There is some evidence to suggest that the south-west end was originally closed, ending up against the natural rab.

The passage floor slopes gently downhill and has a drainage gully cut into it, originally covered with flat stone slabs, which links with drains in the round chamber and entrance passage. This drainage system still contained Iron Age

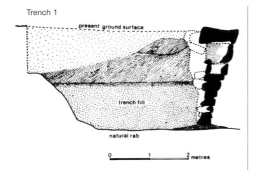

Trench 1

present ground surface

trench fill

natural rab

0   1   2 metres

Trench 1 section (see fogou plan, page 35)

pottery belonging to the early phases of
the settlement which had been missed by
the previous excavators.

Further down the long passage a well-
built opening on the right can be seen near
the south-west end. This gives access to a
steep, narrow *Side Passage* ('creep') leading
up to the surface. Excavation has shown
that it was built of six uprights, three on
each side, set on the sloping sides of a
trench cut into the rab. Four uprights
support the very large central capstone and
two support the lower lintel, with dry-stone
walling in between. (The combination of
walling and uprights creates a 'cupboard'
remarked upon by Borlase and others.) The
upper lintel, which is carried on horizontal
wall stones, is best seen from outside. A
path can now be followed from the south-
west end of the fogou, passing behind the
cottage wall, and up the steps on the right
by the boundary hedge. From here the
upper opening of the 'creep' can be
approached. Looking down from this point,
it can be seen that the stone-walling of the
fogou passage ends in a vertical face. (The
last capstone here was replaced during
excavation.) It has already been suggested
that the fogou ended up against the natural
rab at this point. The trench cut into the
ground beyond, along which the path runs
to reach the steps, is thought to be later
and indeed excavation has revealed a deep

sump here (now filled in) dug during some
phase of the settlement.

This sump-digging activity may have
resulted in the south-west end of the fogou
being breached. (The occupants of the
cottage could have re-used this sump as a
well.) It seems likely that by Phase IV of
the settlement the fogou consisted of a
through passage, open at both ends, instead
of the originally closed structure with
access only down the 'creep', and possibly
through the opening in the south wall
opposite the round chamber. At a later
date the passage was deliberately filled up
to the roof with earth, from the round
chamber entrance down to the south-west
end. The round chamber itself and the
eastern end, however, were left clear.
Borlase had the task of removing this
infilling of earth, in which fragments of
Iron Age and Roman pottery were found.

From the position above the fogou, the
north-west part of the site may be visited.
Little can be said about this area since it
remains to be excavated at some future
date. Note the later boundary wall
(Boundary Wall I on the site plan)
immediately north of the 'creep', and
further to the north-east the gravelled area
above the Round Chamber. This part was
excavated and occupation material found.
The curved wall (Hut H on site plan)
surrounding this area was built in several
stages, but may have enclosed a 'house' at
one time. The paved opening through this
wall on the north-west is hard to
understand, since it appears to lead straight
into the pit for the Round Chamber. This
suggests that the latter was floored over,
perhaps forming a 'cellar' to the house
above.

The remainder of the houses can now
be visited by first walking down beside the
eastern boundary wall to the site entrance.

House A

This was the first house to be examined, in

House A: an oval stone house typical of the second and third centuries AD

HOUSE A

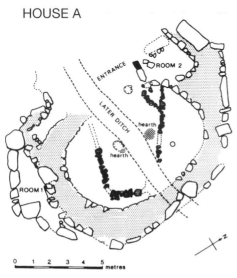

Plan of House A

1964, when it appeared before excavation as an irregular oval setting of large granite boulders. Although by no means intact, it proved to be the best preserved of all the houses in the village, and the only one in which hearths survived as well as most of the stone covers to its drainage system. The lowest course of the enclosure wall is well preserved and a slight step up on the north gives access to a small 'room' within the thickness of the house wall. A second compartment added on to the south side may have been part of the house or have served as a shelter for stock. The house, which belongs to the group of smaller enclosures like House E and House III, was certainly occupied in Phase IV though its constructions may go back into Phase III (see chronological chart on page 27).

House A is bisected by a flat-bottomed *ditch*, thought to have been built as a drain or boundary (or both) round the southern part of the site after it had been abandoned. The walls of the house had been roughly reconstructed over it on the east side, and on the west, where the entrance is thought to have been, no trace of house walling survived intact. As can be seen from the plan, this ditch also passed through House B and House E.

From House A the boundary wall can be followed along the flat ground on the south which has been cultivated in recent times. Note on the right the partly excavated House B over which a terrace wall had been built abutting the side of House A.

Before visiting the next enclosure, House E, mention must be made of an earlier house further to the north, of which only gullies, post-holes and traces of floors remained. These have been covered over with turf, and are therefore not visible, but the position of the house – House A1 – is marked on the site plan, partly overlain by House A and House B.

House A1

It can be seen from the plan that a semi-circular gully, on the north (uphill) side only, demarcates a house 24ft (7.3m) in diameter, with six posts to support the roof. Two of these post-holes were located by excavation beneath the wall of House B. The house walls may have been built of turf or wattle, which would account for their disintegration after two thousand years, and the entrance appears to have been on the east. Floors of clean rab survived in the centre and also much burnt material. Plain flared-rim jars and sherds of roulette-decorated pottery date this house to the second century BC, though occupation appears to have continued into Phase III. This is the only house of its kind in the village of which the ground

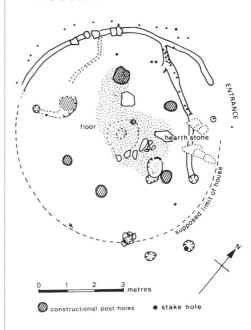

Plan of timber-built House A1

plan could be established, though others must have existed during the early phases of the settlement, and an attempt has therefore been made at a reconstruction drawing (see page 25).

House E

This house belongs to the group of smaller oval enclosures in the village such as House III, with which it compares most closely, both in size and construction and also in having a large stone with a hollow, set into the floor. The occupation is thought to have begun in the first century BC/first century AD (Phase III) and continued during Phase IV. Owing to the disposition of the stone-covered drains, it is thought that the entrance to House E and to House F further north, were on the west. There is no evidence as to how the two houses

HOUSE E

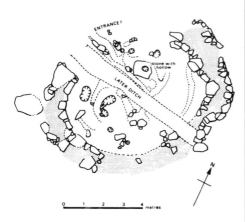

Plan of House E

were connected, in the absence of intervening walls, nor whether they were in fact part of a larger courtyard house complex. Both dwellings appear to have been floored, wholly or partly, with white kaolinized granite, traces of which were found in the excavation, especially where protected round the base of the walls. A kaolin floor of this type was well preserved at the neighbouring site of Goldherring and the material was clearly popular, with good reason since the smooth white finish was not only durable but must also have looked attractive.

House F

Walls immediately north of House E represent the remains of another house, or part of a house, designated House F. The turfed area between the surviving walls had been cultivated and most of the archaeological features had been disturbed. On the south-west, cultivation reached down to the natural rab and destroyed the evidence so completely that excavation was not pursued in that direction.

North of House F lies House III and in fact the two house walls are bonded

together here with clean yellow rab and are believed to be contemporary.

House III

This is one of the better preserved houses on the site. It belongs with the other smaller oval enclosures such as House E and House A and was occupied mainly in Phase IV, though traces of earlier occupation were also found.

A good paved entrance on the south-east and a paved area on the north, leading up into House II, can be seen. Holes for internal timbers, (probably roof supports) a fire-reddened pit for cooking and drains round the sides and down the centre were also uncovered. Note the large flat stone with a hollow in the centre, between the paved area on the north and the entrance on the south-east. When discovered, this hollow contained a rubber of fine-grained greenstone and the stone is thought to have been a quern for grinding cereals and other foodstuffs. A similar stone with a hollow in it can be seen in House E.

In the empty area between House A1

HOUSE III

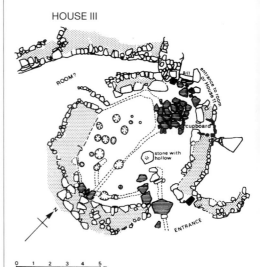

Plan of House III

and House III was found a rectangular pit (not visible, but marked 'grave?' on site plan) covered with four stones similar to large drain lids. A small plain pot lay inverted in one corner, but otherwise the pit contained nothing but a filling of dark earth and some clay at the base. It is thought, however, that it might have been a grave, perhaps of a child, but all traces of the body would have long since vanished in the acid soil. Another interpretation is that it served as a latrine pit. In either case, it was the only example of its kind found in the excavations.

Proceeding up the slope from the west side of House F, leaving the croft hedge on the left, the next house to be encountered is House IV (now turfed) which shares party walls with House III as well as with House II, vividly demonstrating the way in which houses interlock with one another on this site.

House IV

This house is one of the three larger enclosures and has a diameter of over 40ft (12m) from north to south. It has few features of a typical courtyard house and there was little evidence of the compartments or rooms so characteristic of these. Much of the occupation within the enclosure belonged to the earlier phases. The sub-rectangular structure on the north is not an original Iron Age feature, but was built more recently as a shelter for animals. Note the vertical revetment slabs to the fogou on the left beyond this 'pigs crow'. The south-east side of the enclosure is the best preserved part, the walls on the west having been virtually destroyed, probably when the cottage was built. Traces of pre-courtyard house occupation (Phase II) were found in the enclosure and timber and turf houses probably existed here, though their plans could not be recovered. A fine, deep bell-shaped pit, lined with white china clay and intended for storing grain, was found.

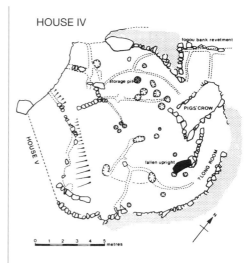

Plan of House IV

This was in use during Phase II–III but filled in and floored over later, probably in the Roman period. Such pits are rare in Cornwall, but are well-known features in the Iron Age economy of southern England. Drains with stone covers and rab floors over them survived on the west side of the enclosure, where the entrance is believed to have been, and numerous pits and post holes were also found in this area, at a slightly lower level. Further occupation, with paving, gullies and pits, continued under the cottage wall and is named House V on the plan.

From the west side of House IV, the small post-medieval croft may be visited.

Cottage

This two-roomed cottage had a central doorway, a small window in the back wall and a paved terrace on the south side. A central staircase or ladder would have led to a room upstairs. (A less ruined but similar cottage at Botallack, near St Just, has a large undivided upstairs room in which a miner's family of ten were all known to have slept in quite recent times.)

Ruins of the eighteenth-century cottage

In the west wall is a stone fireplace, originally an open inglenook with granite slabs at the sides, spanned by a massive granite lintel which would have supported the stonework of the chimney. Cooking was probably done over an open hearth rather than in an oven. The roof may have been of slate or, more probably, thatch. A small privy or washplace is built against the outside of the east wall and has a stone-covered drain leading from it.

The cottage is thought to have been built around 1750, on analogy with similar well-dated houses on Samson, Isles of Scilly, and was occupied for about 50 years, judging from the pottery and metalwork found. Some use of it was also made during the first half of the nineteenth century, with pottery dated to 1830–50. During this occupation, probably connected with mining activity, the fireplace was modified and the washplace was built. The cottage was abandoned and already partly in ruins, having lost its roof in a gale, when Borlase examined the fogou in 1867.